FIRE DANGER RATING TODAY

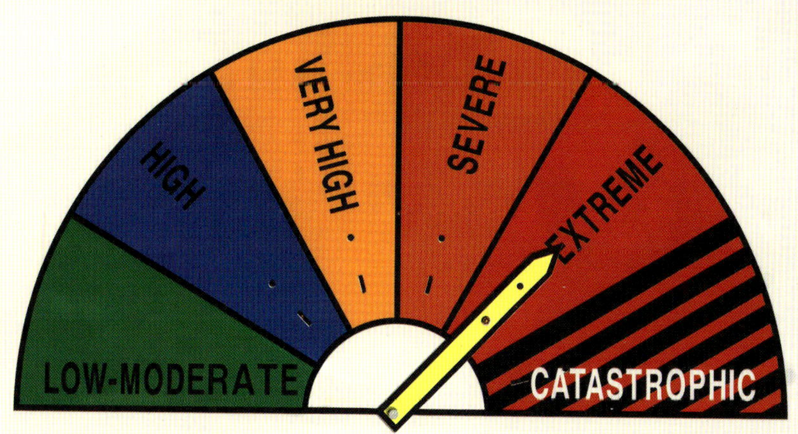

PREPARE. ACT. SURVIVE.

The First People hunted across grasslands. There were many patches of grasslands across the country. The first British explorers saw the First Peoples setting fire to large areas of tall grasslands. This is called Fire Stick Farming!

These fires allowed green grass to grow. It stopped the forests from growing and kept the country as grasslands. When Fire Stick farming is stopped, the grasslands grow into forests very quickly. The dead grass and forest leaves build up on the forest floor. The trees spread to the grasslands, and there is no food for the kangaroos.

Black Thursday was the first terrible firestorm in the new colony. In February 1851, the fire burned across a quarter of Victoria. Many people lost their homes, farms and animals. Many people also died. This painting was created in memory of the Victorian Black Thursday victims. Why did the forest burn so hot and across so many lands? Was it the build-up of grass, leaves and trees after the First Nations' People stopped Fire Stick burning?

Australia has had many terrible bushfires. Every year there are bushfires in Australia. Homes, farms, animals, and sometimes people, die. Children lose their homes, and many native animals are killed. The country is burned so badly that it takes a long time to grow back again.

NSW RURAL
FIRE SERVICE
NSW RURAL
FIRE SERVICE

These terrible bushfires start easily if the weather is hot and dry. Some summers are very hot and dry. The forests and grasslands easily burn. It is difficult for koalas and other native animals to escape and run from the fires. Much of the wildlife is injured during a bad bushfire. If they are lucky enough to escape the fire, they may still have the problem of losing their habitat.

The people fighting the fires use many things to help them. It is very dangerous to try to stop bushfires. The firefighters are very brave and hardworking people. Most of the country firefighters are volunteers. These volunteers work long hours to save houses and farms. They receive no money for their efforts and some are injured by the fires. If not for these wonderful volunteers, the bushfires would be so much more destructive.

TASMANIA
FIRE SERVICE
1319

Helicopters are used to carry large loads of water. The helicopter drops water on the fire. They work to protect houses and people during a bushfire. The helicopter can sound a siren to warn people below to move away from the water coming down. It also tells people to run from the fire. These helicopters can work very long hours from dawn until dusk during bad bushfires.

ERICKSON AIR-CRANE
N243AC
741

Firestorms sometimes jump ahead of the firefighters. Burnt tree leaves fall from the sky. These are called embers and they can start new fires. Embers can travel a big distance. In firestorms some embers have travelled 20 to 30 kilometres ahead of the fire front.

To stop fires spreading, the firefighters may start a firebreak. This is also called back-burning. The firebreak is usually made along a track and is designed to stop the larger fire. Sometimes, if the wind and heat is too strong, this does not work. Firefighters can also create a firebreak by dropping pink fire retardant from a large, specially designed plane. This foam slows the fire and prevents it from spreading to homes and towns.

RURAL FIRE
BRIGADE

Fire stick burning is still practised in many parts of Australia during winter. It may help in slowing the big fires when it is hot and dry. The burning off stops lots of dead grass and leaves building up on the ground. Fire stick burning may help to stop huge bushfires in summer. First Nations' People still burn their own country to get new grass growing which helps to feed the wildlife.

If the fire does not burn too far into the ground the grass will regrow quickly. The grass may grow back in weeks. These new shoots feed the kangaroos, wombats and other animals. If the fire is very hot, it will be many months or years, before the grass grows back.

Word bank

Australia	injured
vast	habitat
sections	helicopters
patches	firefighters
grasslands	dangerous
British	volunteers
explorers	receive
kangaroos	kilometres
Victoria	firebreak
colonial	usually
terrible	wonderful
difficult	destructive
koalas	retardant
	specially